or-ity®

From Idea to Author-ity®

Write, publish, and promote a non-fiction book to market your business.

By Dixie Maria Carlton

From Idea to Author-ity®

Copyright Dixie Maria Carlton 2017© All rights reserved.

Except for the purpose of reviewing no part of this publication may be reproduced or transmitted in any form or by any means, electronic or mechanical, including photocopying, recording or any information storage or retrieval system, without the written permission of the publishers. Infringers of copyright render themselves liable for prosecution.

Disclaimer:

Every effort has been made to ensure this book is as accurate and complete as possible, however there may be mistakes both typographical and in content. The author and the publisher shall not be held liable or responsible to any person or entity with respect to any loss or damage caused or alleged to have been caused directly or indirectly by the information contained in this book.

Published by Maria Carlton Pty Ltd
Yatala, Qld, Australia www.mariacarlton.com
ISBN: 978-1544196145
Printed by Create Space, an Amazon.com Company

From Idea to Author-ity®

Dedication

To Anna... who pushed me to always focus on getting through what needed to be done. "Birthing a book is just like raising a child – the hardest days sometimes offer the best potential for great rewards".

From Idea to Author-ity®

From Idea to Author-ity®

CONTENTS

Introduction	5
1: Planning and Writing Your Manuscript	13
2: Finishing the First Draft	18
3: Pre-Press and Production	23
4: Book Design	33
5: How to Get and Use Great Reviews	42
^: Printing Options	46
7: The Publishing Industry	63
8: Publicity	73
9: Distribution	82
10: Talk It Up	89
11: Online Marketing Options	94
12: Using Social Media to Promote Your Book	109
13: Get Ready to Sign Copies	111
BONUS CHAPTER:	
- Using WORDPRESS as your Website Platform	117
About Dixie Maria Carlton	129

From Idea to Author-ity®

Introduction

"You just don't know what you don't know...
yet!"

I personally love this saying – because in the instance of writing and publishing books, for first time authors it exactly sums up the mysterious journey that lies ahead on the path to becoming an '*author*-ity'.

I'm not sure why I'm still surprised when new writers say things like: 'but this is such a great book, how do I get it into onto Amazon?' or, 'I just have to get an agent and then the rest will be easy', or words to that effect. Another one I constantly come across is the author who thinks that the easier option will be to simply create an e-book instead of a 'real' book.

Even the original version of this book was intended to be 'just an ebook' but there are a million

From Idea to Author-ity®

books of all varieties that are abandoned on computers and in landfills that attest to the fact that any kind of book still needs to be properly written, edited, formatted, designed and then marketed. That's before you even get into the issues of distribution.

The hard truth is, there are already a number of authors who have written about *your* subject - some good and some bad; some wealthy ones and many who are sadly sitting on the boxes of their unsold books instead of furniture now. There are no new ways to become wealthy, paths to enlightenment or management techniques. They are all mostly the same as someone else's version of it, but told with fresh stories or examples. So the world is not waiting for *your* words - sorry. But, if you have the wherewithal to back yourself and your message and turn your material into a book (either digital or printed) and do it well, then you have a chance at getting your book looked at seriously by any number of publishers, agents or book sellers. You just have to know how the system works - from idea

From Idea to Author-ity®

to finished product and then how to get it out to your market.

Some people do fluke it - but you know, even the most successful authors in the world often received enough rejection slips to wallpaper a small office with before finally hitting the literary jackpot. I don't believe in flunking it - you really have to be exceptionally good (or know someone who knows someone - wink, wink) to be able to bypass the alligator filled moats and drawbridges that guard most publishing castle gates.

Note: Celebrities are a whole other story!

So - what do you need to know about publishing in order to have a real shot at making it?

Here's a list of 10 things - but it's out of 100 and these are just the basics. These rules are the same whether you work with a traditional publisher, self publish or want to do e-books.

1) Get a good *book* editor to go through your manuscript and make sure it is AWESOME, not just 'pretty good'.

– 9 –

From Idea to Author-ity®

2) Work with a book shepherd or industry specialist who knows how to get the book from manuscript to 'ready for publishing'; whether that means ready to self-publish or ready to submit to a traditional publisher.

3) Know who your target market is, why they would want to buy your book and what they might pay for similar books on the same subject.

4) Find out who else is writing (well) about your subject.

5) Have a reason for writing the book - not just because you want to make money as a writer, because most likely you won't!

6) Be prepared to speak and promote your book yourself - your publishers won't do a lot, unless you are paying them to and/or you are already very famous and selling millions.

7) Learn how to sell from the platform and use public relations and social media to get your book promoted.

From Idea to Author-ity®

8) Join some relevant associations and submit articles and blogs to their magazines or websites so that you can get your book some direct attention from those who might be interested in your topic - ie your target market.

9) Create a website and make sure it's professional and geared towards promoting your book and your expertise as an author and speaker so that people can go there to find out more about buying your book and/or tapping into your expertise in other ways (beyond your book).

10) Learn how to creatively position yourself in your market, to promote your work within your genre. Get smart about your personal marketing and personal brand.

Working with an agent is only likely to happen if you have really outstanding ideas, quality material and a very well prepared manuscript and/or completed book which has already got a proven track record of sales.

A big publisher is only likely to look at your work if you can get their attention and that means having

From Idea to Author-ity®

a great agent who loves your work and will promote you well, or a book which is topping the charts already.

If you are a new author, you owe it to yourself to learn all you can about how this industry works, how other authors have succeeded and what's made some books stand out successes in your genre.

I first wrote this book back in 2011 for all the authors who were embarking on their journey to write and publish a book. But even in the last five years there have been some significant changes in the publishing world, and so this updated edition is now based on the knowledge I've gained over more than 40 books (mostly non-fiction) I've published/nurtured, or helped come to life since 2006.

I sincerely wish for you to use this information to assist you in getting your book from inside your head into the hands of your market, easily.

– 12 –

From Idea to Author-ity®

1

Planning and Writing Your Manuscript

Here's one easy way to layout the book's subjects so that it flows easily from one subject to another within your book.

Start with a blank piece of paper. Now map out the following grid:

Even if you are not specifically going to have your book divided into parts 1-3, these give you the framework for where each part of your book might go.

For example, if you are writing a book about small business help, the first part would be about accounting, the second part about marketing and the third part about hiring staff.

From Idea to Author-ity®

		Introduction	
Pt 1: Accounting	1: Using Accounting Software	2: Business Planning	3: Tax Management
Pt 2: Marketing	4: Traditional Marketing	5: Online Marketing	6: Customer Services
Pt 3: Employees	7: Finding People	8: Keeping People	9: Firing People
		Summary	

Write up what each 'part' is about. Then, decide what the three main chapters will be about part. Using the same example, you might have part two (marketing) as chapters (4) Traditional marketing, (5) Online marketing, and (6) Customer services – which then segues well into 'Part3', People. Chapter seven therefore might be about the importance of hiring the friendliest and most helpful people for the front line of your business.

From Idea to Author-ity®

Write the working chapter headings into each of the soft-squares of the grid.

You may end up with three chapters for each part, with a short introductory chapter for each (ie, a total of 12 chapters) or you might have only nine chapters, and each might be separated as 'Part 1, 2, 3'.

You may also find that your book needs16 or even 20 shorter chapters. It will depend on you and your content – this plan allows you to get an idea of that framework before you start writing. It will also give you a clear outline of how the book will flow when it's finished.

The other great thing about using this layout plan is that you can also use the same system for planning each chapter, with subheadings for articles you wish to write. It's all a matter of scaling it up or down according to the size of document you intend to write. It's a very good way of organising your mind map branches.

One other thing to mention: don't write your book in chronological order. Instead, select which

From Idea to Author-ity®

chapter you wish to write next, and we recommend tackling the easy ones first. Once you get to the half way mark, it will feel easier to keep going and finish your manuscript. If chapter three is particularly hard, or needs a lot of research, then by the time you finish it and still have seven more chapters to go, you may well be feeling de-motivated to carry on. But if you left that tediously long or laborious one till last, you'll know that you've nearly finished anyway.

This grid system is also very helpful when working with other authors on joint projects. You can all decide on the general layout of the chapters, and then select who will write each one, agreeing to swap them over when finished to check (and add to) each other's work.

One of the best things to do is to NOT start writing until you have the plan in place. Often someone will come to me with a completed manuscript and there are some big parts that too long and some too short, or the readability and flow is lacking.

Ideally you will end up with each chapter, having about three or four sub headings, and each of those will be 500-700 words long. This means each chapter is going to be somewhere between 1500 –

From Idea to Author-ity®

2500 words and your book will be anything from 24,000 to 30,000 words.

This roughly translates to 120-160 pages depending on layout, graphics and images used. If you can commit to writing 2,000 words per week, you'll easily have your first draft completed within three - four months.

From Idea to Author-ity®

2

Finishing the First Draft

You're nearly there. The writing is now completed, and while there may be some revisions and updates required after your editor has gone through your manuscript, you are now at the stage of preparing to print your book. However – it's not just a matter of taking a WORD file to your printer. There's still work to be done.

Review Content

Once you have completed the preliminary draft of your manuscript, that's the best time to turn it over to someone else to take a good look at it. That person may not be your publisher or book shepherd or editor, but they should be able to give you some

From Idea to Author-ity®

good feedback on your content. What you are looking for at this stage is completion of content.

If you are co-authoring a book with another person, one way to ensure good flow of content is to each select which parts you will focus on first, write those, and then swap over so that the other person can review and add content as needed to each section.

With that feedback you can go back and complete what you need to add in to your manuscript, give it another good review and then, hand it over for editing.

Edit content

A formal edit, using a good *book* editor will highlight any discrepancies in your text such as repetitive or missing information, errors, what needs to be referenced, and whether there is good readability and flow to your text.

Your editor will often make whatever corrections are needed, and then highlight the comments or areas that need you to re-do or sort out, and give the manuscript back to you for finishing. You may need

From Idea to Author-ity®

to repeat this process, depending on how much your editor has recommended changing or updating.

This is not a final edit and there are likely to still be many errors and things needing correction before your book is ready for printing – so don't worry too much about spelling mistakes or missed commas at this stage. Just continue to correct anything you see that needs to be fixed as you go, and ask anyone else who might also be checking your manuscript to do so with a red pen or highlighter.

At this stage, before the book is handed over to the pre-press department, the manuscripts (and however many copies there are) will have corrections that need to be updated and checked off in a final copy – the easier you can make this process the better, and using pencil or black ink can be harder to spot on a printed file than coloured pens and highlighters.

Finalise Content

Give your manuscript another check and then when you are *completely* happy that it is completed

– 20 –

From Idea to Author-ity®

in terms of what's in it, and that most of the grammar and spelling checks have been done, it's time to sign off on the manuscript and get it to the Pre-Press stage.

This whole process may take as little as 4 weeks, or as long as a year – depending on your own need to keep re-writing (trust me it happens more than you'd imagine) and your editing team. I say team because there is more than one kind of editor involved at this stage.

Copy Editor
Reviews the content in raw form, advises on readability, mistakes, references required. From there a reasonable amount of re-writing or updating may be required.

Proofing Editor
This person is more likely to pick up all errors, closely review the grammar and spelling and polish the contents.

Final Proofing
This needs to be done by a completely fresh pair of eyes – after the book has come back from the pre-

From Idea to Author-ity®

press stage of being typeset. Sometimes the typesetting may result in an occasional word being dropped or repeated, or formatting errors. This is best done by someone who is not a copy editor because often they will want to contribute more thoughts on re-working parts of your book and you should be well past having to make those decisions at this stage.

From Idea to Author-ity®

3

Pre-Press and Production

Check references, and then double check them again, so ensure that they are accurate, and that each is consistent in the way they are presented.

Illustrations and Diagrams

Determine what style of illustrations, diagrams, photos or coloured images need to be included, and where they will go. Do you need someone else to create them for you? If so, what style will they be in? You have options of hand-drawn illustrations, clip art (not recommended), photos and what you can find on the internet.

Beware of copyright issues related to use of images and diagrams. If you use photos from the

From Idea to Author-ity®

internet, check the status regarding what you are and are not allowed to use. If you have commissioned something to be created or photographed for you, and paid for that, then you own the images. But if you are using something from any other source there could be a range of copyright restrictions, such as where you use them, how you use them, limited publication rights and more. This is an area where you must pay attention to the fine print when you download something you think you've paid for. Take for example the author who really liked an image he used for his book cover, only to find out after it was published that if he sold more than a certain number of books, he would have to pay a *lot* more for the use of that image.

If you have created diagrams and special images which are particularly relevant to your work, but could easily be used by other people, then it's worth talking to an Intellectual Property specialist lawyer about obtaining trademarks and extra copyright protection.

From Idea to Author-ity®

You own your material and therefore automatically own the copyright to it. However, there are precautions you can take to ensure that someone on the lookout for what you have created is further restricted (or at least thinks twice about it) from just taking it and using it at theirs. As stated before, if you have any doubts or questions about intellectual property, I recommend you seek the services of a good intellectual property lawyer.

Foreword

A foreword is what you ask someone else to write as an introduction to your book. An introduction is usually written by you, as a preface to the contents and to outline what the book is about. Also, note that this is spelled as 'fore' with an e – a commonly misspelled word that is worth getting right in your book.

Be selective about who you ask to write a foreword. This is considered an honour by most people, and you want to be sure you ask a strongly relevant person to do this for you. Ask yourself 'why this person' and be sure you know the answer. Some

From Idea to Author-ity®

people when they know you are writing a book will offer to write a foreword and they may not be the best option for your book.

A non-fiction book with a foreword by someone who is closely associated with the topic, and has some weight and credibility within the industry is your best choice. Avoid having this just be 'someone famous' for the sake of celebrity. For example, a book about raising children may have a better foreword by the Children's Commissioner, or the mother of 8 children, than Oprah Winfrey.

Introduction

An introduction is not to be confused with a preface or epilogue. It may be that you also ask someone else to write an introduction for your book – but more commonly you will write this yourself. Your introduction will simply be a 500 – 1500 word summary about what the book will cover, the sort of things addressed in the various chapters, so that the reader knows what to expect from the book. A preface and epilogue are generally found in fiction books, and are pre-story pieces.

From Idea to Author-ity®

It is not necessary to have an introduction or a foreword and many books have neither or only one or the other. This comes down to personal preference by the author, although some editors will suggest the need for an introduction based on their perception of how easily the reader may get into the book without one.

Dedication

Most books have a Dedication. This is the couple of lines where you thank your mother, spouse, children, or inspirational person for their input or being part of your life etc. This is not usually more than one or two lines. The Dedication goes at the front of the book – usually just before the contents page.

Acknowledgments

The acknowledgements are what you might think of as your 'Award Acceptance Speech'. This might be one or even two pages of thank you messages to those people who helped in some way to get your book written and produced. You may like to thank your spouse or significant other family member(s)

From Idea to Author-ity®

for giving you the encouragement or the peace and quiet to write, but you are also most likely to use this space to thank the researchers, editors, sounding board people, mentors, employees, your business partner(s) or coach. I recommend being generous with your praise here, and don't forget the important people who did contribute to your book in various ways.

You should also thank the reviewers of your book here; those who went through it and gave you feedback – both the formal and informal reviews. (See *Reviews* section).

Disclaimer

The world is filled with people who like to write challenging feedback on everything from political speeches to rising prices, and so there may well be someone who fronts up with some feedback on your book one day, who takes delight in pointing out a misspelled word on page 63, or who considers your advice to be all he or she thinks they need to change their lives or revolutionise their business. It is therefore important to add a disclaimer which

From Idea to Author-ity®

absolves you of responsibility for any reader's interpretation of your work. The disclaimer is the paragraph inside your book which explains that:

Every effort has been made to ensure it is as accurate and complete as possible, however there may still be errors of both typographical and in content. The author and the publisher shall not be held liable or responsible to any person or entity with respect to any loss or damage caused or alleged to have been caused directly or indirectly by the information contained in this book. (This is a fairly standard Disclaimer used on many non-fiction publications.)

This should be more than enough to prevent anyone from trying to sue you or your publisher for action the reader may take as a result of your shared wisdom which might result in their business taking a downturn or their children or pets not behaving in a certain way etc. This states that you have checked your facts (and you most definitely

– 29 –

From Idea to Author-ity®

should have) and the reader's interpretation of the contents is their own, and not your responsibility.

Table of Contents

Ideally keep your table of contents to one page only. You may have lots of great subtitles for each chapter, but consider for example if I'd used subtitles as part of this book's table of contents, then it would be six pages long. Remember, people want to *get into the book*. The table of contents is helpful for anyone wanting to just dip in to sections but your subheadings throughout each chapter will make it easy for readers to find specific sections within chapters.

Glossary

A glossary is a collection of alphabetized terms and their meanings at the back of your book. They are especially important in the case of technical translations and marketing books and should also be used for any local, or industry book too.

Index

An index is simply to reference mentioned terms and names throughout the book, and which pages

From Idea to Author-ity®

they are found on. For example, you may have the term 'depression' found throughout a book on mental health, as follows:

depression – 12, 15, 46, 47, 48, 65, 81, 91

medicating depression 12, 46, 48, 91

You may choose to only list the main word, but in some very technical books, your readers may prefer the extension too.

There are some programs which will create an index for you automatically, however, we recommend leaving the creation of your index to the very last of your tasks when finishing your book, and that you check the references are all correct. It is one job best left to fact checkers and those with a love of detail.

About the Author

This is the part where you as the author can profile yourself, your business, and/or your ongoing availability for the reader to access and how they can reach you. You're best to include your website, social media sites, and services you provide in this part of your book.

From Idea to Author-ity®

Remember – the main reason for writing a book is to profile your knowledge and experience as an expert to your market, so use this page (or two pages) very well and put your best marketing foot forward. If you are uncomfortable writing your own promotional copy about yourself, this is an excellent time to hire a professional copywriter.

4

Book Design

Internal Layout

While all these things are being done, your book will be in the hands of one of the most important people of all – the designer and typesetter. This may be one or two people. Some designers also take care of the typesetting and in some cases, the designer is a separate person altogether. I'm going to refer to them as being one person for the sake of simplicity in this book, and refer to them collectively as 'the designer'.

Finding a good designer is important. There are some aspects of book design that are quite specific to books that are different for magazines and websites or other forms of graphic design. Your book designer needs to have some skills and experience with the book industry and know how to create a great cover – and that often means being able to get a feeling for the book itself, and understand who it's targeted at and therefore how to reach them visually.

One great place to source a good designer where you can also see samples of their work is online. www.Fivrr.com is an online source where various service providers such as designers can link up with those who need their services, arrive at an agreed price and terms of business and then you pay for what you get once you're happy with the work. It's usually very affordable, and reliable.

Fonts and Internal Layout

There are great books, and average books, and some that are just plain ugly and hard to read. I'm talking about the aesthetics of the insides of a book. Your choice of font, size and range of headings, margins, and headers can all contribute to making a book easy and reader friendly, or something that most people have to really work hard at reading, and therefore struggle to enjoy.

From Idea to Author-ity®

Whether you have been to a concert, or attended a pottery class, along with the content, it's the smooth running of the show, with regular stimulation that makes it something you'll enjoy. It's the same with books.

Here are some ways to achieve this:

- It's important to not have pages of unbroken paragraphs. Break them up with subheadings.

- Add some diagrams, images or illustrations to help make your book more interesting visually.

- Put quotes into a special space, bigger text, and/or in italic fonts so that they stand out, but only if you have a regular number of these throughout your book.

- If you have special excerpt and information, then put them into consistently formatted boxes or shaded background blocks.

- Ensure you have a reasonable amount of white space, with text not going too close to the edge of the pages.

– 35 –

From Idea to Author-ity®

- Place easy to identify chapter headers at the top of each page.

- Don't mix your fonts and size of text up too much. Stick with simple, clean easy to read, easy on the eye styles of text.

- Fonts for your regular text should be 10-12 pt depending on the style used. Avoid small font sizes, as this can be frustrating for many people even with good eyesight. Better to have slightly larger, than too small, and spread the spacing between lines and paragraphs well so that if necessary, you have a higher page count, than erring on the side of squashing your text up to save paper. Your readers will thank you for it.

Engaging a professional book designer will help to ensure you don't get someone testing silly and unworkable – 'but gorgeous' - styles in your book. Some designers simply get carried away and that's fine in magazines and brochures, but not books – unless it is a very 'creative' style of book and subject and that is your point of difference.

Less is more when it comes to book formatting in most instances.

Front Cover

Some book covers are essentially bold text on a background, and others have photos or diagrams. Different styles of book and various fonts and colours will appeal more, or less, to some people. There is an art to this. Make no mistake, it takes a lot to get the best cover in many cases, and sometimes the 'right cover' will just be the one that a great designer comes up with first. I've known some books to have half a dozen covers tested, and then finally 'the best one' just happens, and other books have been: *'thanks - the first cover was brilliant'* and we went no further in the testing or design phase. Every book is different and there is no rhyme or reason to it – but having a very good experienced book designer definitely helps.

The best way to get your cover design sorted, is to find out what you like in other books, and then discuss this with a book designer who can cater to your requests. Don't ask an inexperienced designer

From Idea to Author-ity®

(of books) to play with something they think is 'cool'. Remember your cover is the first sales pitch for your book, and needs to reflect the content, as well as be bold and inviting.

When you are happy with one or two designs, test them on a selection of your target market. This may mean standing on the street for half an hour each at a couple of locations and asking people to give you feedback and state their preference. Get them to tell you what they both do and don't like about the options. Don't say you are the author, as often they won't tell you what you really need to hear, or you end up engaged in discussions about writing books that are simply time consuming and take you away from your particular mission – to ask as many people as possible for feedback on your cover design(s).

Back Cover

Unless it's the latest 'hot book' of the moment that everyone is raving about it, your readers will want to read the cover to confirm in their mind that

From Idea to Author-ity®

they wish to buy the book, so the back cover is particularly important to get right.

Description

A subheading at the top, very well written 'sales' copy of one or two paragraphs, some bullet points, and a couple of brief raves about it from prominent reviewers. You may also like to ensure a small piece near the barcode and ISBN that specifies the genre so that when your book is being stocked in the shelves of a library or bookstore, there is no confusion as to where it should be. For example, a book title of *Escaping Quicksand* might be about either avoiding bankruptcy (financial self help), working smarter (business non-fiction), tramping in the great outdoors (Outdoor adventure), or it could be a crime novel. You can't rely on sales people who are not familiar with your book to know where it goes unless they have the time and/or presence of mind to read the back cover, and they often don't have either.

A good back cover is not too cluttered with information, looks clean and is well written. Engage

– 39 –

From Idea to Author-ity®

someone with experience to help you with this if you are unsure. *It's well worth getting it right!*

International Standard Book Numbers

ISBN's are a cataloguing tool used worldwide to identify every book published. These are obtainable from the National Library's in most countries, and are FREE in NZ and Australia, but charged for in the USA. You simply call and ask for one. You may have to describe your book project so that the correct type of numbers are issued, and if you are a publisher, you may request blocks of numbers.

These are unique to each and every book in the world, and your responsibility by having an ISBN is not to get the book to market – you may even decide not to print more than enough to give selected clients or friends – but to ensure a minimum number of two copies of your book are sent to the National Library in the country of ISBN issue for cataloguing. This also ensures that your book is registered on the international published books register. This means that your book can be located by anyone in the world who might have a particular

From Idea to Author-ity®

interest in your subject via a massive internationally connected series of databases.

You may also be surprised to find that your ISBN is not only unique to your book but enables it to be searched by the international network of libraries all over the world. Once a book is in the ISBN system, it is searchable anywhere by this unique identification number and publishers take great care to ensure each book is carefully catalogued.

Bar Code

A barcode can be issued against the ISBN by your printer on request and usually costs well under $100. Your printer will often be able to supply your bar code.

If you are producing your book with Create Space, they can supply both the ISBN number and the Barcode for you if required.

From Idea to Author-ity®

5

How to Get and Use Great Reviews

I was publishing a book for a man we'll call Allan a couple of years ago, who got all enthusiastic and sent his nearly finished book off to someone he knew reasonably well - and had some minor celebrity status, and in Allan's view, was a great person to have rave about his book. He called him and was very excited about the feedback he got from this man and decided his testimonial was perfect for the back cover.

When asked to check that his associate was happy with the way we'd put his words on the back cover, (a final check before printing) to Allan's surprise and embarrassment the man said that he hadn't realised Allan was going to do that. He said that the feedback he'd emailed to him were for

From Idea to Author-ity®

Allan's own personal use, not to be bandied about to the rest of the world.

This sort of thing actually happens a lot. The other thing that trips up the review process is giving your finished manuscript to someone – after it's all been laid out and looking lovely – and they don't understand that you only want a comment or quote about the book, not suggestions for a re-write!

Six steps to getting great reviews for your book:

1. Decide who you want to review it – and then understand that just because you ask 20 people does not mean you'll get all of them respond. It's worth aiming for 3-6 reviews, and you get more than that then use the not quite so glowing or powerful ones on the book's website and marketing platforms. A powerful endorsement quote is not necessarily going to come from Oprah or Tony Robbins, or even other top ranked celebrities just because you may know them. Instead, the best ones will come from those who have positions or other books which mean they are well qualified to comment. For

– 43 –

From Idea to Author-ity®

example, a book about child safety, with an endorsement quote by the Minister of Child Services or a family Court Judge, may carry far more weight than Tony Robbins in the minds' of the readers anyway.

2. Ask them if they would be willing to review your book. Be sure they know that you intend to use their comments – and possibly in condensed or edited format – for marketing purposes, and that may include being quoted on the book itself.

3. Set a timeline by which you need their response.

4. Provide a list of pre-prepared short quotes and invite them to either use any of those you've supplied or to take them as inspiration for their own words. This makes it so much easier for many people who do struggle to find the right thing to say, or to understand the type of thing you require.

5. Get them to put it in writing that they expect no payment for this review and endorsement, and that they will accept your right to edit their comment.

From Idea to Author-ity®

6. Send them a signed copy of your book when it's printed.

This is a system of getting reviews which can help make it very easy for other authors, celebrities, or experts to agree to review your book. When used correctly this can save you the embarrassment of printing comments about your book that are not signed off on, or their purpose is misunderstood by the reviewer.

6

Printing Options

Before your book is ready for printing you will need to decide on which of several options are available to you. You can have it printed in a traditional sense, paper, ink; hard copy or paperback, or you may wish to create an e-book. Well there's even more to it than that, and the first part of the process is determining exactly how you intend to get it to the hands of your prospective readers, and by knowing who they are, how they most prefer to have your book.

Many people are loving the idea of having all their books on readers such as Kindle or iPad. Just as many still seem to want to pick up and thumb through old fashioned pages. The thing to remember is that you can do both – you are not

From Idea to Author-ity®

limited to only one option here. But let's look at these options in more detail, and help you to understand what you need to do for each.

E-Books

There is more to producing an ebook than just typing something up on your laptop and saving it as a PDF file. For an e-book to actually be that, it still needs to be edited, typeset, designed, have a cover, and an ISBN number. In fact, the only thing that really separates a quality printed book from a quality electronic book is how it's delivered to the reader – online or on paper.

That's not to say that many people don't still think that taking shortcuts on e-books is acceptable, but seriously, if you have gone to the trouble of writing a good book, edited it, ensured it's looking good and of high quality in either style, then it's worth doing a good job of the final production phase. And not only will your readers thank you for the time taken to do so, but your quality publication will stand above others that look like the poor relations by comparison.

– 47 –

From Idea to Author-ity®

You can of course produce your ebook by turning it into a PDF file, but for it to have wider scope and appeal to your market, you'll also wish to have it converted into files suitable for a range of electronic *Readers*. The reason for converting into a '*Reader*' friendly option is so that the book automatically fits the size of the *Reader*, and the pages flow easily and at the right sizes as requested by the reader of your book.

Convert to E-Pub

There are a range of software options, and online websites where you can simply upload your text, word or PDF file and have them converted to an 'E-Pub' file, which can then be read by: Apple iPad, Barnes and Noble Nook, Kindle, Sony Reader, BeBook, Adobe Digital Editions, Lexcycle Stanza, BookGlutton, AZARDI, Aldiko, WordPlayer on Android and the Mozilla Firefox add-on OpenBerg Lector. The ones most common at the time of writing this book are the **iPad, Sony Reader, Kindle, and Barnes & Noble Nook**. There are others that come and go – but if you are going to

– 48 –

From Idea to Author-ity®

cater to the masses, these are the ones most likely to be used by your target market.

There are also specialist e-book distributors online – most specializing in particular genres such as fiction or non-fiction, and these may be of interest to you. However, remember why you are writing a book and who you wish to target.

For the purposes of reaching your target market and ensuring they understand your specialist knowledge and services, the most likely options you'll choose are to convert your book to an E-pub file. If you do wish to convert to an e-pub version, I recommend getting help from someone who is an expert at this.

The cost of converting your book to an E-pub file is likely to be anything from 'free' to several hundred dollars, depending on how much work is necessary to customize your e-book, and whether you are comfortable using online resources and software for this yourself.

One of the things that's changed a lot in the past few years is how easy it is now to upload

– 49 –

From Idea to Author-ity®

your books to Amazon through Create Space and Kindle.

Ensure that if you are creating an e-book version of your book that you do embed relevant hyperlinks and images, perhaps even video and audio files where appropriate. These bring additional flavour and value to your book.

P-Books

Printing your book on paper is still a very good idea for most non-fiction books and here's why:

- They are more easily shared and loaned to friends and associates.
- These books more than any other genre are likely to be kept, along with notes and highlights put there by the reader.
- P-Books are more easily sold or handed out as a tangible item *of value* for marketing your services.

One thing that might work very well for you is to have your book printed, and offer a printed book, with the E-book version made available to your online purchasers. That way the purchaser gets the instant gratification joy of having the book immediately, while still having the P-book turn up a few days later.

– 50 –

One thing that Amazon allows you to do is make the Kindle version of your book free or very low priced if the reader purchases the printed version too.

Paper Printing Options

If you are printing your book, then you'll need to decide between Print on Demand (POD), Digital or Offset printing.

Offset printing is the traditional print methods used for many years, where the file is transposed into plates, each of the four colours to be printed (Magenta, Cyan, Yellow, Black) are separated and printed separately overlaid on each other to get the highest density of colour and quality. The pages are laid-up usually in 12 or 16 per flat sheet, run through the printers very quickly, and then collated, cut to size using pre-set crop marks set by the designer, and finally then the book is bound together.

If you are printing more than 1000 copies of a book, this is usually considered the most cost efficient and highest quality option for printing it.

From Idea to Author-ity®

For less than 1000 copies – or in some cases it's worth considering at 500 – your next best option is to digitally print the book. Using machines that are like very sophisticated photocopiers, the book can be printed straight from the computer file, on individual sheets, then collated, trimmed and bound. These are suitable for as few as one book at a time or many, because the sheets are usually fed into the machine as A4 or A3 size.

As digital printing presses are becoming increasingly sophisticated, the covers and laminating can also be done easily, and the quality is sometimes very hard to distinguish from offset to the untrained eye. However, the drawbacks are still a lesser quality than gained by offset – especially for colour printing – and the cost is higher per book than offset printing is in larger quantities.

Having said that, the quality of POD books coming from companies like Create Space are excellent. And it's a very user friendly system for authors to use.

From Idea to Author-ity®

POD is about printing the book – even in as small a quantity as one at a time – when someone asks for it. The cost is quite high per book to produce, but the upside of this is no need to warehouse spare copies. When an order is placed, the book is produced on a digital printer and dispatched to the purchaser.

When seeking a quote from a printer, be sure to specify whether you wish to have offset or digital printing; many printers will offer both, but just as many specialize in one or the other.

Your QUOTING Checklist

- ☐ Size of Book – Exact Dimensions
- ☐ Number of Pages
- ☐ Paper Stock – *insides and cover*
- ☐ Colour, B/W or One Colour Alternative?
- ☐ Hard Cover or Paperback?
- ☐ Laminated Cover – Matt or Gloss?
- ☐ Binding

Size

You can print in any size at all, but there are economies of scale to be considered with some sizes. For example, if you are offset printing, there

From Idea to Author-ity®

may be additional wastage by printing in 'odd' sizes, or with shaped paper (ie a round or hexagaonal book) which would require a die-cut mold.

Number of Pages

If you are printing in Offset, then remember the sheets will be fed laid-up as 12 or 16 pages per sheet of paper. It is best therefore to ensure your book is finished up to be in a number divided by 12 or 8. It's best to have your designer discuss the printing specifications with your printer to avoid additional wastage or ending up with lots of blank pages at the end of your book.

Paper Stock

Most printers will encourage you to see paper samples before deciding on one you like. However - if you are new to this, it will pay to remember that most inside pages will be printed on 95 – 110gms weighted stock, and most paperback covers for offset will be 250-350 weight stock, and most digital printers will offer 180-250 weight stock for covers. Don't let a printer try to sell you very expensive and heavier paper for printing your book unless your book is intended to be a very beautiful coffee table

From Idea to Author-ity®

or gift book that should most definitely have heavier paper. You can easily overspend on this part of your project if you are unfamiliar with paper weights and qualities, and we recommend finding someone to help you with this if you are unsure about your printing quote details.

Colours

You will be asked to specify if your text or the insides in general are black and white, or any other colours. You may wish to print the entire book in navy blue or dark red rather than Black ink – but you will need to specify this as 'one colour – navy blue' if so. Otherwise, if the entire insides are simply printed black, then you can ask for One colour b/w.

If you have colour images or text throughout your book, your entire book will need to be treated as a *full* colour print job – which is a lot more expensive than *one* colour – however if you only have 2-4 colour images, or photos all in the same place, (ie middle or split evenly in some other way) then these would be printed separately to the rest of the book and collated after printing, before binding.

From Idea to Author-ity®

The most important thing to note here is that you MUST discuss your book with your printer before quoting it, so that he or she knows exactly what is required.

Seek recommendations for printers from other authors or industry contacts, to find a printer who is used to dealing with books like yours. And we recommend seeking no more than three quotes – as printers in most areas (either geographically or industry specific) talk to each other if there's a quote going 'right around town' and you'll not gain anything more than annoyed printers if you attempt to get a LOT of quotes for comparison. You'll also likely find yourself confused by different jargon and quote layouts that way too.

Laminating

Even if you want your book to be a matt finish, you'll need to ask for it to be laminated, so that the cover lasts longer than the first time the book is read. One of the fastest things to give away a book has been self published and cheaply produced, is by a cover that is not only badly designed, but too thin, and curls, frays at the edges and gets finger marks

– 56 –

From Idea to Author-ity®

all over it. Laminating your cover protects it and gives it a much better finish visually too.

Some digital printers do not offer this, but it is well worth insisting on.

Binding

The most common types of binding are saddle-stitched, which is stapled through the centre, and is only really suitable for booklets. There is also a saddle stitched and bound option where the sections of the book that have been offset printed are collected together and stitched (with a thread usually) and then bound together using a glue binding these sections to the spine. This is the most robust option for book, also the most expensive and not offered by all printers.

The other option is perfect bound – where the pages are all flat set (guillotined) and glued into the book spine. This is the most common, and you are likely to be offered this option for your book. However, there are varying degrees of quality in this option, and a good perfect bound book will stand the test of time (and many repeat readings) but in

– 57 –

From Idea to Author-ity®

most cases of short run books that are not above 300 pages, this is perfectly adequate. If you are unsure about which type of binding best suits your book, discuss it with your printer.

A Word on Kindle E-Books

There is a slight variation in how you will need to prepare your Kindle E-book for upload than the Createspace upload options. For one thing, as an E-book you are not allowed to have any blank pages, but you are less restricted by specific dimensions as you are with a printed version. You are also able to easily edit the content of your E-book after it's published should you need to whereas it's much more troublesome to do this with your printed version.

Because your printed version is going to be far more carefully typeset than your Kindle version, it is best to separate the book files into two separate ones after the final editing phase and before the final typesetting phase. Treat them as two different books in terms of proofing and layout from that point. You can of course give them the same cover and all the other parts of the pre-press process are the same, apart from the ISBN number and barcode.

However, the back cover text is not required for the E-book, but should be used at the *Book Description* when uploading it.

Your PRODUCTION Checklist

[ ]	Review Convent
[ ]	Edit **Content**
[ ]	Finalise and sign off content
[ ]	PRE-PRESS
[ ]	Check references
[ ]	Confirm/find/contract illustrations/diagrams/photos
[ ]	Arrange **Foreword** to be written
[ ]	Write **Introduction**
[ ]	Write **Dedication**
[ ]	Write **Acknowledgements**
[ ]	**Disclaimer**
[ ]	**Glossary**
[ ]	**Index** created

From Idea to Author-ity®

- [ ] **Index** checked
- [ ] **Table of Contents** checked
- [ ] **About Author** written
- [ ] Pre-print reviews obtained
- [ ] **ISBN** # ordered
- [ ] **Bar Code** obtained
- [ ] **Front** cover checked
- [ ] **Back** cover checked
- [ ] **Spine** checked
- [ ] Print prices obtained
- [ ] Print files checked and approved
- [ ] Files uploaded to printer
- [ ] Kindle Version created
- [ ] Kindle Version uploaded

Once your book is published, you can also send it to editors of other publications for review, but you don't always have to wait for that, and pre-printing advance copies specifically for review is an option to consider.

From Idea to Author-ity®

When your book is *completely finished* and looks like it's meant to, you have some quality reviews, and feedback from peers, then it's time to do a final edit - this time for grammar and punctuation. A last sweep through by someone who knows how to proof at a very high quality level. This person will most likely not be the same person you used for the content editing, but a 'fine tooth comb' detail person who's great with a red pen, but knows not to try and re-write the contents. He or she will also pick up on things like whether references have all been checked, that the index numbers are correct, and that any odd things in the layout are identified.

While one proofer will take responsibility for this, there may be others at this stage who also check the book for you, to ensure that everything is double and triple checked.

However, please bear in mind that the chances of your book being 100% error free and totally faultless are never guaranteed. I've known books to have been checked and rechecked up to 20 times and still a reader has come back to the publisher or

– 61 –

author and commented on tiny troublesome things like a double 'and', comma out of place, or a two-wide gap in some text.

If you accept that your book most likely won't be perfect, but that 98% is a great target to aim for, then your book is likely to get to market sooner, and will give you less stress in the final stages of birthing it. However, that is not to say that you should accept anything less than a commitment to the highest possible quality for your book. Obvious and plentiful mistakes that will have your readers running back to you in droves to point out the faults in a book are a very unpleasant thing for any author.

One extra piece of advice I'll offer is to set a deadline and commit to getting your book out by that date. If you keep stretching your deadline, it is likely to make you more inclined to keep altering the contents, adding and changing things, and in these instances some books can take two years to reach completion when they were in fact perfectly ready more than one year beforehand.

From Idea to Author-ity®

7

The Publishing Industry

It's relevant to mention the publishing industry and how it works and why your focus should be on using your book as part of your marketing strategy, rather than trying to get sales happening through the retail stores.

The publishing industry has changed a lot over the past 100 years, and even more quickly since the development of the digital publishing age. How books are sold, and what returns and margins are standard, how the book distributors and literary agents work is explained in this chapter.

The book industry has been in a state of flux for well over a decade now. The book store chains are mostly found in malls, with high rents and therefore a need to focus on quick turnover. This means that

From Idea to Author-ity®

best sellers and those books which have strong marketing and public relations strategies behind their launch are going to be a lot more attractive to book sellers than non-fiction books by new or unknown authors.

The non-fiction genre has some advantages and some disadvantages when it comes to the distribution of books. The biggest disadvantage is what commonly called a 'long tail'. Simply it works like this:

A novel, cook book, or biographical work of someone relatively famous is likely to have a fairly high immediate return, peaking somewhere within the first six months of a book's launch. A business book, or non-fiction inspirational book is likely to peak at about 12 – 18 months, and sustain a reasonably long duration of steady sales, but in smaller numbers per month. For example, a business book might be still selling an average of 100 copies a month after five years, having peaked at say 5,000 copies (in retail sales) at say nine months after release – so 6,000 overall. A popular

From Idea to Author-ity®

cookbook might have sold that many in the first six months, and maybe 1000 over the next five years in total. For retailers, the faster turnover is more attractive and therefore better focused on. This means that back catalogues of some genres are reliant on independent book sellers, and what you the author can sell directly by other means.

The reality is that very few retailers will ever sell books directly for an author, and therefore a distribution service is required if you are serious about trying this option. Unfortunately, very few distribution agencies will handle one-off books by unknown authors.

Why am I making it sound so hard to get your book into general retail distribution? Simply because it *is* hard to do - a frustration exercise for most authors, and very unrewarding financially.

Your reason for writing your book must be remembered when it comes time to consider such things as distribution of it. While it's a nice idea to have your book sold through bookstores, the reality is, it's more trouble than it's worth. The returns are

From Idea to Author-ity®

very low (usually only 35% of RRP after taking out distribution and booksellers margins – which might mean it's only pennies per item), and make the whole process of what it takes to get a book into stores very unprofitable.

If you think about why you decided to write a book in the first place, then go back to considering who your market is, and what you want them to know about you, your information, and how it will affect them.   Use your book as a giveaway, to open doors and get people wanting your consulting, coaching, speaking services.

Sell your book when you speak at events, or on your website.   We'll cover this in more detail in chapter 14.

Use Professional Help

It pays to use professionals, not just your cousin or best friend's younger brother. This is true for a number of things relative to your book, but most important when it comes to editing and design.

Some of these next paragraphs may sound repetitive as I've touched on some of this

– 66 –

From Idea to Author-ity®

information already, but as editing and design are the most complex part of the process, it's worth repeating where relevant to ensure your complete understanding.

As outlined already there are several stages of editing a book. The first is when you have finished your manuscript and are basically happy with your contents. Give it to a group of beta readers - friends or colleagues who understand your subject and are good at grammar. This is a very helpful part of the process of finishing the manuscript and getting some relevant feedback. The next step is to give your manuscript to an *experienced book editor.* Regardless of how well you think you write, an editor will pick up on things that neither you nor your sub-editor friend will have noticed, that relate to the way the reader – your identified target market – will want to read the book.

It may be that there are some things needing to be referenced, or simplified in the way you've explained them. Perhaps there are things that you've written that make complete sense to you

– 67 –

From Idea to Author-ity®

(and the friend who read through your manuscript and helped you to finish it) but that just need either clarity or extra simplification. There are also likely times where you've written repetitively. A good book editor is charged with the task of grooming your raw file and turning it into a reader-friendly book, which has chapters that flow, descriptive text that is just right, and no confusing bits.

A book editor will also correct grammar and pick up on spelling mistakes, but a final proofing will still need to be done. Some book editors are great with the big picture concept of a book and some are great at the details. Very occasionally you'll get one editor who is great at both, but I always recommend using a great content editor and then a separate proofing editor at the end. Fresh eyes always work best when it comes to books.

Also, it's good to use a book editor who is experienced with your particular genre of book. A non-fiction self-help book will be treated differently than a recipe book (more bullet points and lists) or a novel (more dialogue).

From Idea to Author-ity®

The other important step in the process of creating your book is to use a good designer who understands the intricacies of typesetting and designing a book, not just a magazine, brochure or website.

A book's insides need to have a certain number of pages, that fit with the printer's requirements and specifications. For example, a book is usually printed on a set number of pages which when laid up on the machine that prints them, is in multiples of (usually) 16 pages or multiples of eight. So a book that is 144 pages, is laid up in multiples of 16 x 9 pages, but if it's 140 pages, then it's better to be re-formatted to 136, and laid up in 16x8 pages, with a half of one, otherwise you'll end up with four pages blank at the end of your book. A great typesetter who is used to these challenges will often come up with really good options to help make this part easy for you.

Another thing that can challenge a new author who is unfamiliar with the pre-press part of the process is that just simply writing your book in a

– 69 –

From Idea to Author-ity®

program like Microsoft Word, is unlikely to be suitable for offset printing because even though you can convert a finished word file to a PDF file – which the printers use – the crop marks and various other fine tuning is best turned out from using a program like INDesign or Quark.

If the printers prefer using files that have been created properly from their point of view, then the end result for you is that the book is going to look much better.

If you are definitely *only* going to print your book as digitally printed short run – best suited to under 500 copies at a time - then the file produced in Word is not quite so important an issue, because the file is effectively loaded into a giant computer and just printed.

However, an offset printed version of your book – anything over 1000 copies at a time – is treated differently at the printing stage, with your file output creating plates, which are loaded onto an offset machine that prints large multi-sheet or rolls of paper by running it through ink.

– 70 –

From Idea to Author-ity®

An advantage of offset printed books is that the quality is often much better, and the covers are thicker – so they last longer. However, some books are very well suited to the print on demand option of digitally printing only a few at a time.

A great graphic designer does not necessarily create a great book cover, or understand the technical issues of layout for the insides of a book either. They can learn these of course, but don't make the giant mistake of letting your designer friend learn about book pre-press on your book. There's just too much at stake.

You might like to engage the services of a book shepherd to help you work through the many options, especially if this is your first book. He or she will have experienced the publishing process of many books, and be able to help you decide on everything from how to print, what sort of book to produce, how you will sell it, and what recommended retail price you may charge for it if you are planning to sell copies.

– 71 –

From Idea to Author-ity®

Book shepherds also usually have access to experienced designers and editors, as well as having knowledge about distribution and printing options which can help you to avoid some very expensive learning curves.

Your relationship with a book shepherd or publishing coach is important if you've not published before, as he or she will help guide you through the process, with all the traps and considerations well managed before they even become a problem. Most first or even second time authors just don't know what they don't know yet – and your reading this book will help a lot but there is still much to learn.

From Idea to Author-ity®

8

Publicity

Google Books

Google Books is another international directory set up by Google to enable books to be located. Their sales details and reviews are visible online – with links through to sales points – and the first few pages are readable online. This is a very interesting system which enables readers to see what the book looks like, read some of the content, but not copy or print anything of what they can see on the screen.

In order to upload a book to Google, you must have a Google mail account, and then sign up for approval to Google Books. The upload process is relatively straightforward, and you can either submit the finished book for scanning into their system or a PDF, with separate front and back cover pages.

The great thing about Google Books is that you can specify where the book may be purchased, and link directly to those places. If your book is mostly found on your own website, then people are easily directed there to buy it. If you are unable or unwilling to have it available on Amazon.com, then you can still share with people the relevant information you would otherwise have visible, like the reviews, and a peek inside the pages.

Press Releases

A press release will help to ensure that the media knows about your book when it's printed and available through your distribution system – even when not available through retail outlets, you can benefit from a press release to help ensure your market finds out about your book.

When you have great news to share, don't advertise it by paying someone to write an 'advertorial'. Instead write a powerful, interesting

From Idea to Author-ity®

and attention grabbing press release aimed at getting editors and program producers to pick up the phone and want more information. Maybe they will interview you, write a feature, or just reprint what you've sent them, but if they think their readers, listeners or viewers will be interested too, you've got an excellent chance of scooping space in their publication FREE.

Some things to remember when writing a good press release:

- Make the story interesting – not just selfserving publicity. Use a generic angle, don't just talk about how great *you are*, talk about the event, situation, opportunity, product. Be clear, succinct, and don't forget to make it sound BIG – even if you think you are bragging – do it! If you are the only person who's done or doing something, don't hide yourself under a bushel – step firmly into the spotlight, but explain *why* it's of interest to the audience or readers.

From Idea to Author-ity®

- If you are shy about giving yourself a rave, then ask someone else to write the release for you and give them all the BIG details.

- Make yourself available for interviews – put clear contact details at the bottom of the release and invite the recipient of the release to get back to you for more information and/or interview or in the case of a book release, offer to send a review copy and/or excerpts for publication.

- Mention who you are – a brief background or bio – introduce yourself to the editor or producer. Only celebrities who are totally well known household names don't have to do this every time a press release is sent out.

- Don't feel you have to send the release to every media outlet – select only those who might be particularly interested in your news. The media are overloaded with press releases every day – and will block you if you abuse the ability to send you release via online subscriber channels. Be selective!

From Idea to Author-ity®

- Try to keep to only one page – this is a teaser for the recipient. Don't 'serve the whole dish' – promote the best and juiciest bits, and you have a better chance of them coming back for more of the whole story if they are interested.

- Be selective about timing – don't send it too early or too late. Yesterday's news is no longer interesting to anyone but you and tomorrow's news might not even happen.

TIP:

Try to avoid sending your press releases out to electronic media such as radio, tv, and newspapers when there is a lot of other news happening. For example, if a major earthquake, war, or election is threatening, or a political issue is hotly brewing, reporters and editors tend to be more focused on bigger and more urgent news. While this is not always something you can plan around, sometimes you can delay a release until whatever is currently on page one is a little more settled.

From Idea to Author-ity®

Identify media to send your press release to:

Media Selection:		Where:
Electronic Media – ☐ Radio, ☐ TV, ☐ Online publications		
Print Media – ☐ Magazines, ☐ Newspapers, ☐ Community publications		
Social Media – ☐ Linked In, ☐ FaceBook, ☐ Twitter, ☐ Instagram ☐ Pinterest ☐ Online community groups *(remember to put hyperlinks into your release where appropriate)*		
Associations and trade connections		

– 78 –

From Idea to Author-ity®

Your clients and own database	

Check the following:

- Your press release has an intriguing, powerful, attention grabbing headline.

- Don't make it 'all about you' in a self-promotional way but keep the end audience/readers in mind – what is of interest to them? Keep it generic – the release is a teaser which you hope editors/producers will be interested enough in to follow up and interview you for more information.

- Put a clear set of contact information at the end so that editors/producers can contact you and follow up for more information.

- *Proof read and double check the quality of the writing* – remember you are sending this to professional communicators who will not bother to read anything that's unprofessionally presented.

From Idea to Author-ity®

- Finally: Check it again – if you were reading this story in a magazine or newspaper, would you think it was *interesting*, or just *self-serving rubbish*?

Press Release - 11 January 2017:

International Recognition for Local Inventor <Bold headline>

Local business man turned inventor John Jones has been awarded a prestigious contract to supply ....

This is where you write the real story – what's happened, who does it involve, why is it of interest to the editor who will read this – and how can you make it sound compelling and NOW.

Next paragraph is where you put some background to the story or situation.

Summarise the story a little more.

John Jones has been... *<write a 100-150 word outline here and have it proofed before sending>*

For more information please contact John Jones at: <Email>, or <Phone>,

---

– 80 –

From Idea to Author-ity®

From Idea to Author-ity®

9

Distribution

Even before you have had your books printed and ready to launch to the world, you must address the issue of where you are going to sell them, who you will sell them to, and how they can obtain copies.

Printed Books

The way the distribution industry for books works, has always been *mostly* based on this system:

The author works through a publisher, the publisher works through a distribution agent, and they sell the books to the book stores and libraries. It used to be that authors could sell their books directly to book stores (and in very rare cases this

From Idea to Author-ity®

does still happen, but usually only when the independent book store is known personally to the author). Publishers could also once sell directly to stores and libraries, but with the number of books now being produced in all markets, nearly all booksellers insist on only working with distribution agents, and distribution agents only work with authors and publishers with at least a dozen titles.

The reason for these changes is due to simplification of administration. As margins are increasingly squeezed in retail, and by publishers, everyone is trying to be more efficient, and so the process in effect becomes more streamlined with less individual players, but it does mean extra middle men, and therefore extra complication for authors.

The outcome is that unless you have more than a good handful of titles to offer, you are hampered by having to work through other people to sell your books on your behalf, to try and get them into stores and therefore available to your readers.

From Idea to Author-ity®

The margins are also very tight and make this quite uneconomic.

For example:

The book might have a RRP of $20.00 including sales tax of 10%.

$ 20.00 RRP
- 2.00   Tax 10%
- 8.45   Retailers Margin 45%
- 3.60   Distributors Commission 20%
$ 5.95   Net return to author. Or if you are working with a publishing company, this might end up as only $0.60 (10% of the net).

If your books are costing you $3-6 each, this is a hard way to make any money out of your knowledge.

If you sell direct from your website, then the difference between what you make out of your $20-$30 book, and what it costs you to print it is considerably better; you could even throw in free post and packaging and your return will still be well ahead of the retail trade option.

Getting Your Book Onto Amazon

One of the first things that people want to know about publishing is how to get their books onto Amazon.

– 84 –

From Idea to Author-ity®

Amazon is a great place to sell your books if you have an international market. However, check the fine print carefully if you are outside of the USA, Canada, and the UK. In order to get paid you'll need to have to have a USA tax code which means filling in a series of forms and extra paperwork to ensure you have all your tax agreements in place. This may sound easy, but I assure you it can take a lot of mucking around if you are not used to tax rules in your own country or the USA. Amazon does provide a lot of information on this on their website, but be prepared to read a lot of fine print, and for it to take time to sort out.

This of course also affects CreateSpace.com and Kindle – which is owned by Amazon.com.

You also used to need to have a distribution system set up in the USA or Canada or UK, if you wish to sell printed books via Amazon.com – because they need to know that if there are sales happening, they can get stock immediately (not from thousands of miles away) to fulfil their order obligations.

– 85 –

From Idea to Author-ity®

Using the POD option provided by Create Space offers a great alternative to this, but there are some cost issues to consider.

Amazon's Royalty Calculator

Royalty Calculator*		eStore		Amazon.com		Expanded Distribution
Use the royalty calculator to figure out how much you'll make every time your book is manufactured.						
		Standard	☆ Pro	Standard	☆ Pro	☆ Pro
List Price	16.00					
Interior Type	Black and W? ▼	Your Royalty				
Trim Size	6" x 9" ▼	$8.30	$10.15	$5.10	$6.95	$3.75
Number of Pages	150	Our Share				
Calculate		$7.70 Details	$5.85 Details	$10.90 Details	$9.05 Details	$12.25 Details

* Figures generated by this tool are for estimation purposes only. Your actual royalty will be calculated when you set up your book.

You can see that you'll make $5.10 per book in royalties for each book you sell on their standard plan. Amazon takes $10.90 per book including the cost of manufacturing it.

Take out withholding tax. Payments are only made when there is >$100 in your account.

If you have a marketing strategy that includes directing people to Amazon.com, then this might we well worth it to explore and sign up for, but if you don't, then your book might just as easily sell a few

– 86 –

From Idea to Author-ity®

dozen a year, and your royalties will be nothing to celebrate.

If you are outside the USA, UK or Canada, you might be better off promoting links to your own website for sales set up and accessible from there.

Other places you can sell to or through:

- **Association or franchises linked to your topic.** Invite them to promote your book to their members, or better, to buy enough to give away to all members as a special promotion.

- **Your clients.** Those you know who will benefit and might also share details of a special offer to their clients. For example, if your book is about accounting for small businesses, ask a selected group of accountants to review the book, and then offer a special deal for them to offer to their clients- this could add up to hundreds of books per accountant – which makes them look good to their clients, and you have an

– 87 –

From Idea to Author-ity®

easier sales process than approaching individual companies.

- **Marketing to your entire database.** And include in this group your online social media contacts, to get them interested in buying your book directly.

- **Selling your book at the back of the room.** When you speak at training or conference events as the guest speaker on your specialist topic.

- **Give the book away to delegates.** Anyone attending a convention you are presenting at and working the cost of one book per person into your speaker fees.

- **Through Print-on-Demand online stores.** This includes Createspace.com, Lightening Source, and Lulu.com

From Idea to Author-ity®

10

Talk It Up

Now that you have a book, you can use this as a marketing tool and door-opener to the organisations you most want to speak at, train for, or consult to. Here's a few things you can do with your book to maximise the opportunities ahead of you.

Send a copy with a cover letter to the person who books speakers/trainers in the organisations you have already determined are a good fit for your expertise. Tell them that you are available for a meeting to discuss their needs and to determine if there is any potential for you to do some business together in the future. Make this all about *them*, not just a rave about you or your book. However, be sure to reference the fact that your new book is

From Idea to Author-ity®

new, and that you've sent a signed copy for their personal library.

Cite a reference to and bookmark any particular chapter that you feel they might find most interesting in relation to their current business or industry issues (making it clear you've done your homework already) and that you are seeking further opportunities to meet if/when the time is suitable to do so.

Follow up with them a week later to ensure they have received your book and letter. There's a good chance that they will at least have checked the chapter you bookmarked. And maybe by then willing to agree to a meeting with you or at least give you a few minutes on the phone answering any pre-prepared questions you may have about their conference plans or training opportunities.

You can offer to send them more information if they agree to receive it, and at the very least, ask if you can keep in touch by calling again in a few months. This keeps the door open even if they are not willing or able to see you right away. Your book

– 90 –

From Idea to Author-ity®

can be the wedge that potentially keeps the door ajar.

Speaking

Do you want to be a trainer? Do you like interaction of workshops and small group seminars, or are you hungry for the big stages and love Keynote presentations best. One of the things you need to determine as you go through your journey from **Idea to Author-ity®** is the best way to work to your strengths as a professional expert.

B.O.R. Sales

Selling from the back of the room takes skill, and preparation. Here are some tips on how to do this well and some things to avoid. Don't try to be selling books after your presentation yourself, when this time is best used to connect directly with people who want to give you their cards or ask you questions. Get someone else to do this part for you, but make it very easy for them. Don't overcomplicate your systems for payments or bundling of products.

– 91 –

From Idea to Author-ity®

Have a clear price point for each item you are selling (if more than just one or two books), and give your audience a compelling reason to buy 'today' rather than go online to order later. They are far more likely to purchase on the spot than get around to it later.

This compelling reason might take the form of a special price, or bundling two or more products together for a premium rate on the day.

One way to make it easy on yourself and those wishing to buy your books if you don't have an assistant to help with this, is to create a form, where the purchaser can simply write his or her name, phone number, and credit card details (complete with name on card and expiry date, plus signature), and simply ask that they work on an honesty system.

The chances are you'll get very few people who will be dishonest when doing this – as many speakers who have tried this can attest to. When you consider the cost of your book and the amount

From Idea to Author-ity®

you might have to pay an assistant, this is a risk well worth taking.

By asking for a phone number you can still contact them later to check any details if something is amiss.

From Idea to Author-ity®

11

Online Marketing Options

You will need to build a good presence online for your book that fits with the position you are establishing for yourself as a professional expert. Start by creating a webpage on your existing site just to promote your book before it's ready to launch.

Start by putting extracts and teasers about your book there and using good search engine optimization techniques based around quality key words that are appropriate for your book so that people searching for the topic(s) your book focuses on can start to find you and your book information online.

Turn some of your longer sections of your book into blogs which are also rich with good key words and

From Idea to Author-ity®

tagged appropriately for SEO purposes. Then spend a few minutes every day posting snippets, comments and media commentary and opinions (appropriately) on your Facebook, and twitter accounts.

Build up a following of people who want to know what you know and how you can help them so that when your book is ready to start selling. You can ensure they know about it through that online reputation you are now working on building up using he mix of social media resources available to you.

Now let's look at each of these tasks in more detail.

Create a Web Page

With your book's own domain name registered and pointing at the page. Talk with your webhost about this to make it easy and straightforward if this is new territory for you.

By registering a new domain name for your book, you can refer people directly to that part of your website without having to worry about extra long

– 95 –

From Idea to Author-ity®

url descriptions. For example, if your book is titled: ACME Great Ideas, you can create marketing messages that simply refer to: www.acmegreatideas.com rather than www.mycompany.com/acmegreatideas.html.
Which sounds a lot longer when you say it out loud.

For as little as $10 per year, you can register your domain name at a variety of hosting sites, and then have your domain name pointed to a particular Web page.

Title

Put the book title and subtitle clearly onto the web page, and make it clear what your book is about if the title is a little ambiguous. In fact, using the title as the URL page title is a very good idea. Search engine marketing experts may recommend using important keywords in the title - let's keep it simple and focus on ensuring people know the title, and subtitle so that site visitors know they have reached the right page.

Two resources you may like to investigate for creating an easy page with strong promotional

– 96 –

options to link to your main website or as standalone webpages are www.booklaunch.io or www.leadpages.net.

Overview of Your Book

Write a quick summary at the top of the page. Ensure that you have covered the key points succinctly and create interest and questions in the mind of your visitor – you want them to keep reading and scroll down the page or click through to more information.

Who is Your Ideal Audience?

What sort of person is going to want to buy your book? Consider what key issues they may have that you can help them to resolve.

For example:

- "Are you struggling with bullies at work?"
- "Do you get nervous about presenting in public?"
- "Do you want to know how to make more money while you travel?"

From Idea to Author-ity®

- "If you have great photography skills, here's how to commercialise your talent."

Choose situations that prospects are already thinking about, so it's easy for them to identify with you. The broader you make these situations, the more likely your site visitor will identify with them. However, don't become so broad you're no longer credible.

Keep it tight – instead of 'Here's how to be a better leader', talk about 'Here's 10 ways to improve your leadership style when dealing with teenagers'.

Benefits ("What you will learn")

List the benefit-oriented results they will achieve from reading the book – for example:

- "Your team will be more productive and engaged in creating higher quality widgets"
- "You can easily sell your stories to magazines using these simple techniques"
- "You'll create more measurable opportunities every day"

– 98 –

From Idea to Author-ity®

The more general your claims, the more your prospects will identify with them. However, again if you make your claims too broad, you run the risk of being seen as not credible. For example, if you're writing about selling techniques, it's reasonable to promise, 'you'll talk to more prospects' but it's stretching credibility to claim, 'You'll sell double the number of widgets every day'.

Testimonials

Insert one or two strong benefit-oriented testimonials about the book – as provided by the people who've read a draft copy.

You could also include relevant testimonials about you and your services instead but it's best to focus on the book first, you the author second. After all, you want to have people buy the book – once they have done that they will get a strong feeling about your level of skills, ability, history etc.

Ensure that your reviewers are also relevant to your topic. It's pointless having a famous wealth coach say great things about your book on raising children when they may not even have children

– 99 –

themselves – no matter how many books they've sold on making money.

About the Author

Write a brief one-paragraph biography of you, and why you have the credibility to write this book. You've already written this content in the book's Introduction, so you can extract some of the text from there.

Include a small head-and-shoulders photograph of you as well at this point on the page.

By the way, even if your Web site already has an 'About Us' page with your biography and photograph, repeat it here so Web site visitors get all the information about the book in one place, without having to click elsewhere.

Give Away a Sample

Provide a PDF file for downloading – make it a powerful chapter from the book.

Make them available here as simple PDF links, so site visitors can click to download them immediately. Don't force them to fill in a form

From Idea to Author-ity®

before they can download it; make the process as simple as possible.

Bonuses

If you're offering any additional products or services for people who buy the book, list them here. This is an optional section, and you don't have to include it. However, low-cost high-value bonuses can greatly increase the perceived value of their purchase. For example:

- Offer the E-book version for immediate download, so they don't have to wait for delivery.

- Additional articles on similar topics you've written.

- Downloadable worksheets or templates.

- Password-protected access to videos or other resources on your website.

Order

Include a link to a secure credit-card ordering process for them to buy the book. If you already have this sort of process available for selling other products on your Web site, of course you simply do

From Idea to Author-ity®

the same for your book. If you don't have any system in place, use PayPal, at www.paypal.com, which is a simple and (now) well-regarded payment system that takes just minutes to set up.

If you are happy to simply send everyone to your Amazon page this is easy – as you then don't have to worry about processing sales and sending the books out to customers. Some authors find this a much easier option and there are a couple of benefits to you in doing this.

If all your online sales are via Amazon, then your rankings as an author and the book's individual rankings are easily listed. This is always relevant when you are thinking global.

When your customers see your book is ranked in the top 100, or 500 in its category on Amazon not only do they see extra value in this, but your Amazon promotional algorithms are strengthened whenever you are in the top sections and so your book is easier to find and identify among those also in your category. People can easily search by topic on Amazon – so your rankings do matter.

– 102 –

From Idea to Author-ity®

Another thing you can do on Amazon is paid promotions where you link your book to others which are popular in your category. For example – you may see where it says – "Other people who viewed this book also viewed __". This is sponsored marketing for authors.

Articles

Create some short articles and blogs from your content. You don't have to re-write from scratch items you've already had edited and have confidence in for their quality. If it was good enough to use in your book, it's good enough to use as an article and submit to other publications.

Aim for 400-800 words per article, with a focus on high-quality content that readers can take away and use immediately. Don't worry about giving away the best content from your book; just give it away and the people who value it will buy the book anyway.

– 103 –

From Idea to Author-ity®

E-mail Newsletter

Use something like Mail Chimp, which is an opt-in newsletter format you can use on your website for people to sign up to, then send them an online newsletter once a month featuring one of these articles. You can include some self-promotion in the newsletter as well, but most of the newsletter is the feature article.

Don't create a separate newsletter just for the book; that's just creating unnecessary additional work. But use the book content to create interest in the book via sending these articles and extracts.

Write a Blog

Once a week put some of the smaller extracts into a blog.

If you don't have a blog yet, get one! It's one of the most powerful on-line tools you have for establishing yourself as an author-ity. Unlike your e-mail newsletter, your blog remains permanently on the Internet, just like a Web site (In fact, a blog *is* a web site).

From Idea to Author-ity®

Serious Internet marketers use formats like Wordpress, which is a great platform for creating your whole website on too – and keeps the blog and the website well connected. **There's a bonus article** about how and why Wordpress is ideal for authors and speakers at the very end of this e-book.

Article Directories

Once a month submit your article to an article directory. Article directories are Web sites for sharing articles (Think 'YouTube for articles'). Anybody can list their articles on these sites, and other people have the right to copy these articles, as long as they give appropriate credit to the author.

There are many article directories available, but we recommend you focus on just one or two. One of the best is EzineArticles.com, and you can search Google for others.

Podcast

A podcast is an audio newsletter. In principle, it's like an e-mail newsletter, with subscribers who opt in to receive messages, and they get the messages automatically when you publish them. However,

From Idea to Author-ity®

instead of receiving articles in their e-mail in-box, they receive audio clips in their podcast software and on their audio player.

Turn your blog into a podcast by recording it as an audio file, then publish it to your podcast. This is a hugely popular option, it's easy to do and there is a large segment of many markets who prefer listening to short audio files while walking or driving.

Because you're simply reading your articles out loud, you don't have to spend extra time finding new material for your podcast.

Create a Video

The next step is to produce a video version of your article (with you speaking to camera), which you publish to YouTube. The way someone talks about something and the way something is read is slightly different, so you want to just practice a few times reading through your words, and then relax, and instead of 'reading it through' discuss the information. This makes it sound a lot friendlier and easier for the viewer to enjoy too.

From Idea to Author-ity®

One way to get around the 'I hate talking to the camera' feeling that many people get when they start doing this, is to seat yourself to be slightly side on to the camera, and make the whole piece look like you are talking to an off-camera interviewer.

Video is daunting for some people, and you might find your first few attempts feel and look awkward. But don't give up, because video is such an important on-line communication tool that it's worth getting good at it.

Special Reports

So far we've only looked at techniques for making use of one article at a time. But we're not done yet – we can get even more leverage by combining articles.

Why not take a handful of your articles and combine them into a Special Report. You might title this 'Seven great ways to...' or 'The three most common mistakes to avoid when _'

Write this in Word and add an introduction promoting you and your business. Include your contact details on the cover or a special page at the

– 107 –

From Idea to Author-ity®

end. Then save it in PDF format and give it away to as many people as possible.

Host Webinars

Start running regular webinars for your network based on the topics you write about. You may have to invite people to be there FREE, but as you develop a following and develop more products and training materials you might also consider offering paid programs using this format. At the end of the webinar, you can promote your book and other relevant products and services.

Webinars do take some skill and practice, so they are not for everybody. However, if you do take the time to learn the technology and practice presenting them, you'll find they are extremely powerful marketing tools.

Even if you're not a skilled presenter, you can run effective webinars, especially because you don't have to design the presentation from nothing – most of it is already in the articles you've written!

– 108 –

From Idea to Author-ity®

12

Using Social Media to Promote Your Book

Don't overlook the importance of using Facebook, Twitter and You Tube for promoting your book. Set up an account for each of these, ensure your branding and user names are appropriate to your book, your own name or your company and include some of your already identified keywords in your descriptions about your site. Also ensure each is linked back to your website, and you can arrange for your blog to be automatically set up to create a post on your Facebook and Twitter pages.

Every time you write a blog, or post an article, your Facebook page, and twitter feed will post a link to it, which as your followers grow in number, will alert them all to your latest offers.

From Idea to Author-ity®

The key to making your social media sites really work for you is to ensure you always post good useful content for those who like what you do, your followers. They will even share and repost or re-tweet some of your best information, further helping you to grow your connections.

The overall thing to keep in mind is to be the expert you are, and ensure you are constantly being that person. To the market you want to work with, the 'go to' expert is the one who demonstrates a range of knowledge and expertise, supported by experiences worth sharing with their market. Be visible, be approachable, and share graciously.

From Idea to Author-ity®

13

Get Ready to Sign Copies

Pulling it All Together

The entire journey of 'Idea to Author-ity for me personally has been a challenging one due to the changing landscape of publishing over the last decade. When I started my company to assist people in writing and publishing their books with the intention of doing a much higher quality job of it than the vanity publishing option, I was one of only a handful of publishers working this way in the world. Now there are many who do this, including many traditional publishing houses – yes even the really big ones – who have developed a division within their company to charge authors for the privilege of helping them to get started as they write and publish their first book. What I've outlined in

– 111 –

this book is based on what I've learned through trial, error, experience, and most of all talking with many authors and publishers – of all types and sizes – through the last 13 years. I've also attended international book fairs and worked with literary agents, sold foreign rights deals, and secured high quality traditional publishing contracts for authors. I've also worked with a small handful of authors who are represented by companies who are considered to the giants of the industry, and found that while the publishing side of things was an easy option for them, the subsequent marketing and distribution was not so well supported after the first few weeks of their books releasing.

I'm passionate therefore about the entire journey – from having that first idea, to becoming an award winning, highly respected authority in your field of expertise. In order to do that, you need to allow for an incredible commitment of time and energy, to want that as an outcome so much that the frustrations of the journey don't swamp your enthusiasm for it, and to be willing to invest in learning new things – or spending money on having

From Idea to Author-ity®

someone else do those things for you sometimes. Becoming an author is an expensive decision.

But here's how it can all come together to serve you.

Write a *really* good book. Publish it on Amazon and any other platforms that appeal to you, get good reviews and monitor your author and book rankings. Support this with excellent social media, blogs and newsletters to your existing contacts, and some advertising. The better your ranking, and more books you are selling, the better you are able to put a great press release or article into the hands of the general media or your industry trade publications and respectfully 'demand' (or at least put forth a very good argument), for them to write a good story about you, your book, and what you have to offer your market. This is just one time – and you can build on this multiple times over – that you can proudly wave your publicity under the noses of the market you most want to work with and capitalize on that to get paid for the expert work you do best.

– 113 –

From Idea to Author-ity®

By writing a book about what you are an expert in, or have advanced knowledge or experiences with, you can easily position yourself as being *the* best person in your field to help solve the biggest challenges faced by your potential market. The easiest thing to do is create a book that really gives value and shares much of what you know, that in turn inspires people who need what you have or know, to request more help from you personally.

You may have a whole team of people you work with – or you may work alone. Either way, when you become an author-ity about your subject, your credibility increases in the minds of those who have read your book. Your team will also benefit from increased requests for your services too – by being busier. But personally, your fees might increase, and so will your chances of speaking to groups about what you do. Your own knowledge about your subject will expand too, as you refine your knowledge even further through researching and writing your book.

From Idea to Author-ity®

If others have written about your subject too, then you will have joined the ranks of those *author-ities* by virtue of having written a book. This won't necessarily mean you are competing more fiercely with them, but perhaps this opens the door to more collaboration with them as you gain a better understanding of the similarities and differences in your individual perspectives on the subject matter.

I hope this has demonstrated just how easy it can be to write, publish and then market a book. One that will clearly articulate to your target market just exactly why they should seek your services - and be prepared to pay a fair and reasonable fee for them (and not a discounted one) - because you are an expert at what you do.

Use your book to open doors, continue to expand your knowledge and expertise, and keep learning how to leverage that too.

Most of all, have fun signing copies of your book, and watch out for the readers in airports and cafes who just happen to be reading a copy of your book –

From Idea to Author-ity®

and feel that thrill of knowing you are reaching people well beyond your current networks.

From Idea to Author-ity®

BONUS CHAPTER

Using WORDPRESS as your Website Platform

Wordpress Websites for Speakers and Thought Leaders

As a coach to speakers and authors, who also has a strong focus on marketing, the subject of websites is a hot one and I've assisted in several ways to get speakers' websites up and running from thought to completion and then ongoing maintenance. I'm therefore writing this from the perspective of my own experiences and knowledge, but I will clearly state I am not a *technical* Wordpress wizard.

And this brings me to the first important point I believe needs to be clearly addressed with regards to websites in general.

From Idea to Author-ity®

There are DESIGNERS and then there are WEBSITE DESIGNERS. They are not necessarily the same. He who can do great brochures, may not also be great at online design. I also know a great website design-guy who could not design business cards either.

Rule #1 for getting a new website designed – hire a good website designer.

Another good thing to know is that many designers are terrible copy writers – and vis versa of course. Your designer may not be a good choice of writer, or even project manager for the development of your website.

Rule #2 – consider the people on the team required for the development of a new website.

A great website will most likely have been developed by a team – not just a web designer. Your team should consist of people who have the following skills:

- Design skills

– 118 –

From Idea to Author-ity®

- Technical including coding,

- Copywriting,

- SEO specialist

- Social Media expertise

And maybe a project manager to ensure everything gets done and all parties pull together to produce the best end result.

This brings me to the whole subject of Wordpress as a platform for websites, especially for professional speakers and service providers.

Platforms for Building Websites

Your website needs to be created with something. Options include programs like Joomler, very comprehensive sites might use Magenta, or your website creator might be using their own hard coding program which is sometimes hard to use by others. A problem that has been known to frustrate people everywhere when you might try to change hosts, or take over more control of the site. There are many different platforms used, and one of the biggest frustrations with websites is that as we generally become more technically savvy, we collectively seem to want to take over more direct control of our sites rather than relying on (and paying for) our web-geeks to make all the required updates and changes for us.

Along comes Wordpress, and it's a total game-changer. Suddenly this exceptionally easy to use platform is putting the control back in everyone's own hands, and the cost of creating and therefore maintaining our websites is dramatically reduced.

Wordpress basically started out as a free blog site and in a remarkably short number of years has become the preferred choice of more than 100 million website owners as a free-ware platform.

According to statistics managed by ManageWP, Wordpress sites get more unique visitors per day than Amazon. According to Wikipedia, one quarter of the words websites are hosting on a Wordpress platform.

It took a very short time for even 'hard core' designers to start loving the exceptional functionality and easy use that Wordpress offered

From Idea to Author-ity®

themselves, and the level of power it put into the hands of their clients.

As far as design goes, there are hundreds of design themes, more than 40,000 plugins mean there are literally ENDLESS OPTIONS for making your site look and function the way you want it to.

So where does that leave the designers?

While any one can pretty well log on, start up and create something, using a website designer who is also a Wordpress Wizard is a great idea, because you may still need some hard coding and 'tricky bits' worked out to ensure your site is EXACTLY what you want it to be like. And working with someone like that also helps the stress levels when or if you happen to need technical help any time in the future with your site.

I've personally been working on my own and clients' Wordpress sites for nearly ten years and while I'm very proficient at lots of aspects of the program I rely heavily on a couple of technical experts I can call on any time to ensure all is ok if I'm poking around in the engine room.

From Idea to Author-ity®

You can specify the colours, banner design elements, number of columns, shape and layout of the site you want and then your designer can set that up for you... and that is where the next exciting part of the development starts.

As I mentioned before, your designer may not be the same person as your copy writer, or your project manager. In some companies these teams work together with a client, or in some other situations, the three or four people involved may be external colleagues from different companies who contract into the same projects together. Sometimes it's only two people as the copy writing, design, and project management of the development phase will be shared between the designer and the writer.

The way I work with clients on these is to engage a highly competent website designer who has a general design background, and then I project manage the development and do the copy writing and extra set up parts beyond the actual design and technical set up. I also have another website only

From Idea to Author-ity®

designer who is great at the high- tech, SEO, and basic design parts of a site.

Back to the 'exciting stage' of the development...

With Wordpress, someone who has reasonable technical skills, and who is a good writer or project manager, can take over the balance of the setup of the site once the technical and basic design is completed. That's an indication as to just how easy and flexible a Wordpress platform can be.

For professional speakers and service providers this means that you can easily learn how to manage and update your own site. There are some aspects of the back-end or 'engine room' best avoided by the newbies, but there's not a lot you can't do once you get the hang of it. And that's one of the main reasons why it's become such a popular platform.

Another reason is that there is so much functionality available on a Wordpress site. Plugins are available - these are the optional extras like opt-in sign ups, event tabs, shopping carts, and many more. Many of the plug ins and themes are free too. One great thing about Wordpress is that you site won't get left behind and need to be renewed for technical reasons – as much as a refreshed design will often be a good idea every few years. You can still update with what you have rather than completely starting from scratch each time you update.

Rule #3 – decide how you want your site to look at the start in terms of what theme you wish to use.

This means that having some idea of whether you want a column on one side or two, a boxy look, or maybe no columns at all is part of the early development – changing themes is not straightforward to do once your site is live – in fact that should be treated as a 'new design' mission.

Domain Names and Building Your Site

Setting up your site on a domain name 'www.mysite.com' involves ensuring your site is created on a 'live site' even though the site itself won't be seen by anyone until it's released. Let me explain. Your domain name is the name of your website, and a Wordpress site is created on a platform which is effectively 'live on a domain

From Idea to Author-ity®

name', and therefore you will have already worked out your hosting options ahead of the site being built.

The site can then be built up and made ready for the world to see in a totally hidden way – perhaps with a landing page associated with that domain name that's a fancy 'under construction' page until you take that curtain page away when you are ready to release your site.

Once the site is ready to come out from behind the curtain, you may find there are still going to be things you wish to tweak, change and add, but don't let perfection hold you back. Your site will be something that may continue to evolve for years. It's not always a matter of having to 'build a new website' next time you get inspired to make some changes on your site – you can simply use the ever-evolving opportunities with Wordpress to grow your site through the years.

One more point about domain names – you own them if you have paid for them. Where they are hosted is entirely over to you. Your website host

– 125 –

does not own your domain name (unless you have asked them to register that for you and never paid them for it). You own this, and have complete control of when and where you might want to change its parking garage.

You should expect to pay somewhere around $10-$30 per month for hosting. You might be looking at anything from $500 - $2500 for design and copywriting. And for a project manager service included allow a little more. Essentially, you can have a website that might have recently meant an investment of $10,000-$20,000 for as little as $4,000-10,000.

When you first start to consider a new website using Wordpress as a platform, expect this is going be a 'how long is a piece of string' matter when it comes to cost. But this is all dependent on how much input you need from your designer, copy writer, and project management of the process.

If you are a professional speaker, your use of a project manager might be a good idea if they know their way around a Wordpress back end, and can help bring out the really important information and present it the most effectively for you.

Rule #4 – remember your site can LOOK and FUNCTION any way you want it to – Wordpress is totally flexible.

Search Engine Optimisation

SEO is incredibly easy on Wordpress, because the search engines love Wordpress. Wordpress also has exceptionally easy SEO plugins that make optimizing the site and every page a two minute job.

If you are writing a blog – and you should be – this on Wordpress is arguably much better ranked and found on Google than any other option for blogging. And the best part of using Wordpress for your blog is that it can be all done on the same site – you don't need a separate BLOGsite for your blog – it's all tied together seamlessly.

Disclaimer - this bonus chapter is based on all the things I frequently find myself explaining to my clients about using Wordpress and why I and others I've read about lately feel that Wordpress is a great option for professional speakers to use for their websites. However, I am not a certified Wordpress expert, designer, or website guru by any other name. I am however frequently involved with people who are, and so have a much better than average understanding of Wordpress. If I've misquoted any information above - please feel free to leave a comment and correct me.

From Idea to Author-ity®

From Idea to Author-ity®

About Dixie Maria Carlton

Dixie Maria Carlton is award winning business person, author, presenter, and coach who has been helping professional speakers, thought leaders and entrepreneurs to share their wisdom, and tell their stories as part of their marketing since 2006. Dixie specialises in helping people to bring their stories to life, and on the before (writing), during (publishing), and after (marketing) the book phases of publishing.

Dixie is her first name and the pen name she writes fiction as, while Maria (her middle name) which she is also well known by is her non-fiction pen name. She has a unique background as a top business and marketing coach, publisher, author, speaker and brand communication specialist for SME's and service providers. She's one a handful of people in the world who totally understands the synergy between the speaking and publishing worlds and knows how to help others maximise that connection.

Dixie has assisted dozens of authors to write, publish and in some cases become best-selling authors of non-fiction books. She has also written a number of top selling books of her own, and collaborated on and published several anthologies with writers from all over the world.

Much of her work consists of helping authors working with top publishing companies to get their online and offline marketing, publishing, and speaking strategies aligned for maximum results.

If you wish to know more about working with Dixie for your publishing journey *From Idea to Author-ity®*, please view her contact details here:

www.dixiecarlton.com   www.mariacarlton.com

You can also access her blog and other books via her Amazon Author Page.

Made in the USA
San Bernardino, CA
13 June 2017